THE CHOICE IS YOURS

10 KEY PRINCIPLES TO CREATE A HAPPIER LIFESTYLE

YASMINE BEN SALMI

"LOVEPRENURE"

Award Winning Author

DEDICATION

THIS BOOK IS DEDICATED TO CHILDREN
AROUND THE WORLD.
THIS BOOK IS ALSO FOR ADULTS TOO
BECAUSE I BELIEVE THAT INSIDE EVERY ADULT
THERE IS AN INNER CHILD WAITING TO COME OUT…

Our family friends Tony Jeton Selimi,
aka The See-Through Coach, author of #Loneliness and
mentor to many Wealthy and Famous people, have taught us that
Loneliness and the feeling of unhappiness is two of the biggest
problems in the world today.

The Good News is, that this is about to change for YOU,
IF you choose to practice the key principles that I am about to share.

In this book, I AM going to teach you the
10 Key Principles To Create A Happier Lifestyle.

The question is:

ARE YOU READY?

YES OR NO?

I also want to dedicate this book to my parents
Sabrina and Mohamed Ben Salmi.

My brothers and sisters:
Lashai Ben Salmi
aka Lashai Ben Salmi - My Journey,

Tray-Sean Ben Salmi
aka I'm That KID &
10 Seconds To Child Genius,

Paolo Ben Salmi
aka Pint Size Adventurer,

Amire Ben Salmi
aka Because I AM Intelligent.

Mary Paul
my Nan and Founder of Mary Paul's Creations.

Philip Chan
10 Seconds Maths Expert for editing my book
and believing in me and helping my family and I
to share our books with the world.

FOREWORD

I first met Yasmine in 2014 when she was six and a half (The half is very important to children!). I was at the Mind Body Spirit Wellbeing festival in London writing anonymous love letters. During the event, the whole family came over to our stand and sat down to write letters, Yasmine sat down next to me as I explained to her Mother, Sister and Brother what we were doing. As the rest of the family got on with writing their letters Yasmine looked lost in thought, I asked did she need some help? She said No, I'm ok and started to write a letter she was so engaged in her words and oblivious to anyone else. When she had finished I asked if it would be ok for me to read her letter.

The following words blew me away…

"To you
Happy Celebrations
I am positive and creative
Live Laugh Love beyond your words
Live beyond yourself
Live beyond your words
I am a spirit
I have a spirit beyond
You live beyond yourself"

These powerful words from a 6-year-old! The tears instantly flowed, telling us to live beyond our words, to live, laugh and love! When I read the words aloud to her Mother Sabrina, she was amazed, she asked who told her to write it and was overcome with emotion when I said she had written it herself. This is a lesson we should all learn, to live beyond our words, to put in to action everything we say we will do, to express our true selves at every moment, to live beyond ourselves. I feel so blessed to have had this experience, to connect with the truth being channeled in that moment. I knew that Yasmine would go on to be a great healer with her words, she is an amazing inspirational child, as are the whole family. Those words continue to inspire me to this day, I have even made a feature of the letter on my living room wall.

When I first read this book, I was incredibly moved to see the depth of it for a child, I have ready many self-development books over the years and this covers many of the concepts that even adults sometimes have a hard time getting to grips with. Yet Yasmine writes it all in such an easy way. I believe that Yasmine will continue to inspire children and adults for many years to come and I know that this book will help you to do just that.

Love and Blessings

Sam Livermore
www.sharetheloveletters.com

CONTENTS

ACKNOWLEDGEMENTS

I would like to thank all of my family and friends for being in my life.

A Special Message To You!

Your Health is your Wealth.

'Choosing to be happy will keep you healthy.
Happy thoughts are the key foundation for a happier and healthier lifestyle. What you think about ultimately will comes about."
Yasmine Ben Salmi

Thank you for purchasing this book, there are a few things that I know about you.

First, one of your desires is to increase your happiness.
And secondly, you are motivated to do something about it.

Those two first steps can amount to big changes.
I want to congratulate you and to let you know that by DOING those two elements you are already ahead of most people.

Most people let things happen in their life rather than taking charge, they just hope that happiness will magically come automatically, nor do they take significant steps to make it better if they are unhappy.

Most people are in a RE-ACTIVE MODE, rather than in a REAL-ACTIVE MODE!

Generally, they respond to whatever happens around them. Because of that they are most often in a constant mode of 2 paces forward and 2 paces back going nowhere.

This approach will not create effective results when it comes to creating lasting happiness.

To create happiness, you must be a happiness strategist planning for the future. Not roaming around life responding to what is.
Remember the choice is yours!!...
After finishing my book and taking the actions,
I want YOU to say instead of:

I am going NOWHERE!

I am <u>NOW</u> HERE!
Not <u>NOW</u>HERE!

Did you get what I am saying folks?

A SPECIAL THANK YOU TO:

**Juan Pablo Barahona,
Regan Anne Hillyer** and your team

**Robyn Nikora,
Marisa Lewis, Sunil Chunni,
Sunniva C Holt, Sam Livermore, Sharmila
Soosaipillai, Titi Omole, Ewan Wong, Donna
Hudson, Cheryl Chapman, Giselle Malawer, Andy
Harrington, Tosion Ogunnsi, Douglas
Vermereen, Debie Stoute, Chris Nash, Lily Nash,
Heather Nash, Marie Diamond, Michelle Watson,
Elsie Igbinadolor, Stevan Borthwick, Dean
Williams & Daniella Blechner, Bradley Chapman,
Pastor Nickolas Nunayon,
Narelle Clyde, Lauren Till** and everyone else who
has helped us on our journey

I want to say a big thank you
to our family's publisher

Mayooran Senthilmani & Labosshy Mayooran

Published by
DVG STAR Publishing

Our editor
PHILIP CHAN

Our family graphic designer
PRASANTHIKA MIHIRANI founder of **SWISS GRAPHICS**

You can connect with all of them on Facebook and other social media platforms

I would like to thank everyone who inspires me, encourages me and helps me to become who I am today.

THE CHOICE IS YOURS

10 KEY PRINCIPLES TO CREATE

A

HAPPIER

LIFESTYLE

A MESSAGE FROM MY
HEART TO THE WHOLE WORLD

You are a D.I.A.M.O.N.D. and if anyone tells you that you are not just say:

"I AM A DIAMOND & I CHOOSE TO SHINE BRIGHT"

D –   **DYNAMIC**
I –   **INTELLIGENT**
A –   **AMAZING**
M –   **MULI-TALENTED**
O -   **OUTSTANDING**
N –   **NATURALLY BRILLIANT**
D –   **DREAM BIG!**

Get in touch if you would like to invest in my D.I.A.M.O.N.D. program

Always remember to be kind towards yourself. After all everyone's path to happiness is different.

I have identified **10 Key Principles To Create A Happier Lifestyle** that consistently tend to make life happier and more fulfilling.

I wish **YOU** health, wealth and happiness for this year and beyond.

May you have days filled with unexpected pleasantries in abundance.

FIND YOUR BLISS

HAPPINESS IS NOT a Destination, True Happiness Can Not be found in material things, True Happiness is Not what comes from the outside.

True happiness comes from learning to love yourself and choosing to be happy no matter what.

Happiness is Not
about having a life without problems or having all that we want to do, be and have.

Happiness is a way of life, if we want to live a happy life we need to develop a positive mental attitude. Learning the actions and behaviours that will create happiness and learn that there is no such thing as failure only feedback.

Often adults can live their entire lives without knowing who they really are and not knowing what it is like to be happy.

There are so many unhappy, lonely and heartbroken people in the world.

Everyone's path to happiness is different.

I believe **10 Key Principles To A Happier Lifestyle** can help you to consistently create a happier lifestyle.

The good thing is that things do not have to be like that for you, because you are reading this book.

YOU can choose happiness

There is a reason why I am so excited…

Read on and you will find out the 10 Key Principles that can help you to plant the seed for a brighter and happier future.

Then you will become excited about life too!...

PRINCIPLE #1
JOURNAL

Take a moment to think about the word "EXPRESSION". What does "EXPRESSION" mean to you?

What else?

What else?...

I believe that it is very important to keep a Journal. Because it helps improve your confidence, inspires creativity, helps you to forgive, helps you to heal and improves your communication skills.

In fact, history has shown that many very famous and successful have all kept a Journal to help them by reflecting on their successes and failures, so they can learn from both!

Keep a Journal about your positive experiences will allow you to experience again in your mind, which will also improve your mood. It is always good to express yourself.

The more you express yourself, the more you will heal yourself and learn to forgive yourself and others. Keeping a Journal will heal you emotionally and physically.

Did you know that stress often comes from emotional blockages and over-thinking?

Journaling will free you from mentally being tangled in significant emotional events from your past.

Did you know about the critical connection between speaking and self-expression?

Do some research to see what you can learn. Journaling will improve self-discipline, because you have to set time aside for daily journaling and this is an act of self-discipline.

How to journal

I really believe that you will see the benefits of keeping and writing a journal every day – This is the road to successful journaling.

Simply find a place that feels in alignment and where it feels right for you, somewhere that you will not be disturbed and will feel comfortable to journal.

Always remember to keep it simple and allow your writing to flow, remember to get into alignment and write what feels good and what feels right at the time.

Purchase a new journal with an inspiring image and positive words on the cover, a special pen or a special pencil or both and colouring pens/pencils if you like.

Always remember that you are whole, perfect and complete so just know that everything will work out in the end.

I think that it is very important for you keep your journal private and ask others to respect your privacy.

Your journal is a private and safe place for you to express whatever is on your mind without having to worry about the judgements and opinions of others.

Journal about your dreams, aspirations and present day. Try to journal in as much detail as possible. Write about whatever you feel to, just allow your thoughts and feelings to flow from your heart and onto the pages.

There is no time limit for journaling, you can journal from 1 to 20 minutes or even just one single line or for an hour or so.

Learn to just go with the flow.

At times you may find yourself staring at a blank page and this can be overwhelming, just ask yourself what feels right and what's in alignment?

What is happening in your life?

What are you working on?

What do you desire to experience in my life?

And also, write 5 sentences:

"Wouldn't it be nice if….."

DREAM BIG!

I believe that there's no wrong or right way to journal, so please do not be too hard on yourself.

More importantly just allow your thoughts and feelings to flow.

I really believe that hand writing your journal is important because when we hand write things we use a different part of our brain than typing does.

It's important to dedicate at least a few minutes each day to honour yourself, your thoughts and your feelings.

Writing by hand helps you get in touch with your thoughts and feelings better than typing does.

If you like colour or if you are artistic I think it is a good idea to include this in your journal to make it look fun and colourful.

When journaling it is very important to ENJOY THE EXPERIENCE OF JOURNALLING!

If you are not sure what to journal about, you could start by listing 3 to 5 people who have upset you, and next to each of their names
Write,
I choose to love you because….

I choose to say I am sorry....
I choose to forgive you.....
I choose to forgive myself .....
I choose to say thank you.
I send you oceans of love and a huge cosmic hug 5 x.

Forgiveness is so important and if we do not learn how to forgive and let go it can have a very negative impact on all areas of your life.

You could also journal about 10 x "Wouldn't it be nice if ..." sentences.

Or list 10 x I am affirmations!

You could also list 10 x I value sentences.

You could list 10 x of what you love about yourself sentences.

You could list 10 x of what you are grateful for sentences. I hope these examples help you to get started.

PRINCIPLE #2
DEEP BREATHING

I really believe that our Health, is our Wealth.

Without health, how will you be able to create and enjoy your dreams?

Take a moment to think about the word "HEALTH".

What does "HEALTH" mean to you?

What else?

What else?...

Take a moment to think about the word "WEALTH".

What does "WEALTH" mean to you?
What else?
What else?...

Deep breathing is a very important skill to learn if you choose to create a happier and healthier lifestyle.

Did you know that DEEP BREATHING

- Can help to relax
- Can help you to clear your mind
- Allows more oxygen to enter into your body

4 Seconds

- Take 3 deep breathes and then relax
- Now take a slow and controlled deep breath in to the count of 4 seconds
- And then hold your breath for 4 seconds
- Now breathe out slowly to the count of 4 seconds

6 Seconds

- Now take a slow and controlled deep breath in to the count of 6 seconds
- And then hold your breath for 6 seconds
- Now breathe out slowly to the count of 6 seconds

8 Seconds

- Now take a slow and controlled deep breath in to the count of 8 seconds
- And then hold your breath for 8 seconds
- Now breathe out slowly to the count of 8 seconds

Well done, how do you feel after doing this deep breathing technique?

Stress management is a very important key for creating a happier lifestyle. Stress management can improve your health and lifestyle. I believe that deep breathing exercises are a very, very, very ESSENTIAL DAILY ROUTINE!

Deep breathing exercises can help you to cope with

stress and daily life. It can help you to manage negative emotions better. After all, in our everyday life, we experience different experiences so it is really, really, really, really important to learn deep breathing techniques that will help you to remember that you have a choice, so why not choose happiness.

Do you know what deep breathing exercises does for your body?

It helps your body to get rid of toxins.

Deep breathing helps your lymphatic system function properly, and helps your body to release harmful toxins. Deep breathing exercises are very easy to do if you take the time to practice daily.

It helps your muscles relax. You'll find it much easier to maintain a lot of physical active play when you learn to breathe deeply.

It helps your body to release Endorphins. Deep breathing will trigger the release of endorphins, which will improve your feelings of well-being.

It can help your body to improve oxygen delivery. When you choose to relax and breathe deeply fresh oxygen enters into every cell in the body. This will increase the functionality of every system in your body, concentration and your physical strength.

It helps your blood pressure lower. Deep breathing will help your muscles to let go of tension and your blood pressure can return to a normal level.

INHALE POSITIVITY
AND EXHALE NEGATIVITY

PRINCIPLE #3
GRATATUDE JAR

Take a moment to think about the word "GRATITUDE".

What does "GRATITUDE" mean to you?

What else?

What else?...

I think it is very important to have a Gratitude Jar!

If you do not have one already, you can purchase a Gratitude Jar Set
(Gratitude Jar, Post It notes and Sharpie) from me for only £12.99

I really believe that you should have a gratitude jar because it will empower you to practice gratitude. Did you know that an attitude of gratitude will give you amazing results? And on days when you are feeling unhappy, sad or angry, all you need to do is simply empty out all of your post it notes from your gratitude jar and read all the things you are grateful for.

Remember the tittle of my book
"The Choice Is Yours".

When would it be a good time for you to choose to be happy?

When you have filled up your Gratitude Jar up to the top, you can empty it out and either use the post it notes to make a poster and display it on your wall. Or you can take the post it notes and bury in your garden or somewhere out in nature (because the post it notes are made from water it will decompose) and say momentum, momentum, momentum to ask God/universe for more of what you can be grateful for in life.

The positive energy on the post it will reunites with nature.

Always remember that a negative mind will never give you positive results.

Your Gratitude Jar will help you to practice positive thinking which can transform your life. Always remember that the choice is yours, how can you choose to become a part of the solution instead of being a part of the problem?

Did you know that GRATITUDE can have these benefits?
- Gratitude can increase your long-term well-being
- Gratitude can make you remember happy memories
- Gratitude can reduce feelings of envy
- Gratitude can make you experience good feelings
- Gratitude can help you feel happy on a bad day
- Gratitude can help you to develop a good

personality
- Gratitude can make you feel more optimistic
- Gratitude can help you to focus on how fortunate you are in your life
- Gratitude can help to increase your confidence
- Gratitude can help to improve your sleep
- Gratitude can help you to make new friends
- Gratitude can help to increase your energy levels
- Gratitude can help you to feel good
- Gratitude can help you to relax
- Gratitude make you friendlier towards others
- Gratitude can help to improve relationships
- Gratitude can help to increase your productivity
- Gratitude can help you to shift your perspective toward a person and/or a painful experience

Our mum regularly says to me, my sister, brothers and others 'SHIFT HAPPENS – The question is what are you choosing to delete, distort and generalize?'

Take a moment to think about this…

At times why need to learn to be present and grateful and more patient in life. Change is always happening even when we do not realise

For example:

When a baby is born, they are adorably small and have no teeth but when they get older they develop by growing bigger, they get new teeth, they learn to walk, talk and so much more.

From Amires' (our youngest brother) perspective he wants to be big like us x 4 and grow up quickly.

We tell him that he is a big boy, but he says that he wants to be the same age as us.

From my perspective, I have watched the SHIFT HAPPEN. I have watched as my little brother Amire growing up for the past 4 years.

He has grown up so quickly, he's incredibly intelligent and has an amazing personality.

Always remember that YOU are unique, we all have different perspectives and something worthwhile inside them. We all have something different to add to the world because we are not the same.

I often hear adults say that children grow too fast and that "they lost their cuteness everyday" but all the cuteness is still there and they have just become a grown-up version of cuteness.

Do you realise that you have so much to be grateful for?

Take a moment to think about all that you have been blessed with in life for example the people, the experiences, your health etc. At times, we do not realise how lucky we are until we hear what other people experience for example:

ISSUES FACED BY CHILDREN AND YOUTH

YOU are the future, and it is the responsibility of adults to protect children and ensure that they get the best start in life. Unfortunately, this is not always the case in many places around the world, and including the UK. I have done some research, so take a moment to reflect on the worst situations that children and youth faced with today. It was very hard for me to believe that children experience such bad experiences, but learning about them is a good way to start appreciating our health, happiness, family, friends, love, safety, support, access to education, opportunities and the freedom that you currently have. It also taught me how many things that I use to take for granted, I didn't realize how lucky we were to have hot meals every day. Unfortunately for some children the only hot meal they get is at school, another thing that others may take for granted is food that others throw away in the bin whilst others have to go without food. I ask YOU to think about how your life is different to theirs?

What can you do to help children around the world to improve their quality of life?

With internet access and other technologies available to YOU combined with your skills, talents and **dream**s!

You can become the change you want to see in the world. Trust your highest thought, your clearest words and your grandest feeling.

Your highest thought is always the thought which makes you feel good.
Your clearest words are the words which contain truth and honesty.
Your grandest feeling is **LOVE**.

Around the world children experience: Violence, Indoctrination, Poverty, Life as Refugees, Lack of Access to Education, Child Neglect, Child Labour, Slavery and Military Use of Children etc.

Would these children appreciate having your lifestyle?

Would you like to have their lifestyle?

Here are some common problems that children also experience: Single Parent Households, Growing up too fast, Bullying, Materialism, Obesity and Shifting Economy.

Imagine how different your daily life is to theirs?

What ideas can you come up with to fix some of these problems?

I encourage you to do some research yourself and speak to your friends, family, community centre and school to plant a positive seed to actively contribute towards improving the lives of children around the world and in the U.K.

List 10 things that you are grateful for?

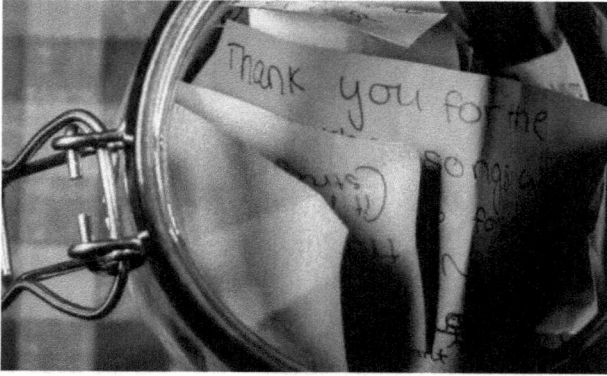

I AM GRATEFUL

PRINCIPLE #4
DECLUTTER

Take a moment to think about the word "DECLUTTER".

What does "DECLUTTER" mean to you?

What else?

What else?...

Do you know how important it is to Declutter and keep your environment tidy and organized?

I think the reason why it is very important to declutter and to keep your environment tidy and organized.
Is because it will allow you to find things easily, an organized mind equals an organized mind. It will make you feel good, it can help you to feel more relaxed, other people will be able to relax in your environment too.
When you declutter, you let go of the old and make space to receive positive new replacements. When you start to declutter and organize your environment, you should take some time to visualise what an organized environment looks like so anytime your environment does not match your vision you can simply make your environment look like your vision. When you start to declutter first, you must be willing to let go of things that no longer serve you.

I really believe that everyone should declutter and keep their environment tidy and organized.

This book is all about finding your happiness and always remember that the **choice is yours**. I believe that "happiness is the key to success". Decluttering helps to clear my mind, it's amazing how our surroundings can affect our mind set. The question is if your home is full of clutter how will your mind feel?

Your mind is likely to be full of clutter too. Just imagine how your mind will feel in an organised environment?

You could feel less overwhelmed and more confidence just by decluttering and organising your environment.

When we declutter our family home, we feel free, we feel happy, we feel amazing and we feel so much more comfortable. When you declutter, you can begin to feel FREE on so many levels. It can help you to move forward and face the future with confidence.

Getting organised and decluttering can help you focus on what matters in life and your purpose. After decluttering I've been able to confidently say NO to things that are not in alignment with me, things that don't line up with my goals and dreams.

When you start to work on clearing things that you no longer need you will realise that decluttering can go on to positively affect other areas of your life.

Before we started to declutter our family home, I felt drained, confused, I had low energy, I felt stressed and overwhelmed, but now I feel at peace.

Did you know that clutter can make you feel tired, dizzy, and it can also make you over eat?

When you declutter make sure you make the process as simple as possible. Only declutter one room at a time. You can start in one area of the room and slowly declutter the entire room.

For example, you could create a room plan or simply visualise how you would like the room to look when you are finished or just go with the flow.

Then select an area to empty and separate items into things you want to keep and things you want to give away to a charity shop/hospice/family/friends etc and you just have to repeat this process over and over and over again until you have decluttered the room.

When you finish that area you just need to organize the things that you have chosen to keep. You can also do this with friends or family if you need a little help.

Good luck – Its time to say goodbye to the Old and welcome the New!

Keeping my space clean, tidy and organized makes me feel good inside.

MAKE THIS YOUR GOOD HABIT!

PRINCIPLE #5
THOUGHTS BECOME THINGS

Take a moment to think about the word "THOUGHTS".

What does the word "THOUGHTS" mean to you?

What else?

What else?...

Thoughts become things, do you know how powerful your thoughts are?

Did you know that whatever you choose to think about, you will eventually bring into your life?

And did you know that you become the average of the 5 people who you spend the most time with?

I HAVE LEARN THIS FROM SOME OF
MY FAMOUS, LOVING, CARING AND
WEALTHY MENTORS

For example

If you choose to focus on negative memories, watch negative images, listen to negative music etc. Then you will soon experience similar things in your life, and the say is true for the **positive** thoughts.
If you choose to focus on **positive** memories, watch positive images, listen to **positive** music etc.

You will soon experience similar things in your life.

This is because your feelings trigger your thoughts your thoughts trigger your actions and your actions repeated over and over and over again create **Results**.

Many people do not know that positive thinking has a lot of health benefits. If you keep your mind in good shape, you'll have an optimistic view of life and that will positively affect your health and well-being in an extremely positive way.

And the same is true for thinking negatively. Because it can actually have an opposite effect on your health and well-being.

Did you know that positive thinking can help you to:

- Live longer

- Fights depression

- Cope better with sickness

- Strengthen your body's immune system

- Cope with stress and hardship

Being able to choose happiness during a difficult period will help you to enjoy life more. After all life without ups and downs is not POSSIBLE, because we always face difficult times as long as we live.

Whenever your mind tries to tell you that you'll not be, do or have something ask yourself these questions:

- Is this mine?

- Does this feel good and is this in alignment?

- What can I learn from this?

It you have a thought that doesn't make you feel good, you can ask yourself who does this belong to me or someone else? If it feels light it belongs to you and then, you simply ask what do I need to learn from this? If it feels heavy, simply say I return to sender with consciousness attached.

I know that I can choose to be, do and have anything I desire. Because I am the master of my mind.

Did you know that every desire you have is also what you do not desire?

Because when you are thinking about something that you desire, you are actually thinking about what you do not desire too. For example:

41

- "I want to be wealthy, is in fact I don't want to be poor."
- "I want to be healthy, is in fact I don't want to be sick"
- "I want to be free, is in fact I don't want to feel trapped"

Did you know that you become a combination of the five people who you spend the most time with?

The more time you spend together, the more alike you will become in your actions, habits, language etc. Your emotions are seeds for your thoughts, your thoughts are seeds for your actions and your actions will create the results you get in life.

I really, really, really, really believe that there is nothing that YOU cannot BE, DO and HAVE

I really, really, really, really want YOU to remember that there is nothing that you cannot BE, DO and HAVE.

It is always a good idea to appreciate who **YOU** are, what you do and all that you have **right now**, because **gratitude** is always a good place to start.

So, take three deep breathes and just relax and enjoy the present.

You Are A Creator

Do you desire to take creative control of your life

journey?

Do you believe that you can have creative control of your life?

How do you know?

Just like my mum used to say to me 'it takes a village to raise a child' and that goes for your future too. Because it takes support to create the future that you want to experience.

And remember, to go into your life and create your dreams. Don't let anyone tell you otherwise and don't let anyone tell you your dream is too big.

Follow your dreams no matter what and trust that 'DREAMS DO COME TRUE'.

My sister Lashai and my brother Tray-Sean have
written a book called
'Kidz That Dream Big
- DREAMS DO COME TRUE'.

Creating is your natural state of **BEING**, so allow your creativity to flow through you.

Choose to relax and simply allow creativity to flow through you so it becomes as natural as breathing. Remember who you really are, so you can reconnect with your natural ability to create and co-create.

Take a moment to think about all the amazing things

you have created and co-created in your life?

When you choose to focus on positive thoughts, do you understand how the amount of orchestration of circumstances and events that have to happen in order to make your dreams come true?

Do you ever stop to think about how loved you are?

Do you ever take time to think about how the whole of life is created to support you?

Do you realise that you are a huge piece to the puzzle, and without you the picture will not be complete?

I want you to begin to understand how blessed you are, how loved you are and how life is orchestrated to support you. I want you to start to look for the evidence of this in every area of your life.

As the saying goes, 'Seek and you shall find'

because will show you the evidence as soon as you start to seek for it.

When you are ready to see the evidence, you'll be able to see just how loved you are, how much of a money magnet you are, how fulfilling life can be, and how much beauty life surrounds you with daily.

You can choose to start your day with positive thoughts, then a positive day is inevitable; it must be. You cannot help but move forward in a positive way when you have positive thoughts, surround yourself with positive people, have positive conversations and take positive actions.

The question is, what do you <u>choose</u> to your attention to?

Whatever you choose to give your attention to will then cause you to emit a vibration, and the vibrations that you give your attention to will go out like an order asking for results that are a vibrational match to the vibration that you are emitting.

For example, if there is something that you desire that you don't have yet.

You should focus all of your attention on having it, what it feels like to have or experience it.

In life, there is a thing called **The Law of Attraction** which means that it will make its way to your reality, because your thoughts are a vibrational match.

But, if there is something that you desire to have or experience that you don't have yet, and you put all your attention on the absence of it.

Then by the **Law of Attraction** will not deliver it to you because in your thoughts you are thinking about it being absent so it will stay away from you.

If you keep thinking the same thoughts and expect different results this known as insanity. But if you want new result you will have to learn to think new **positive thoughts**.

You will have to learn to make the familiar, unfamiliar and the unfamiliar, familiar in order to transform your life.

Learn to master your thoughts, or your thoughts will master you.

Did you know that if you do not choose to think about building your own dreams, someone else will make you think about building theirs?

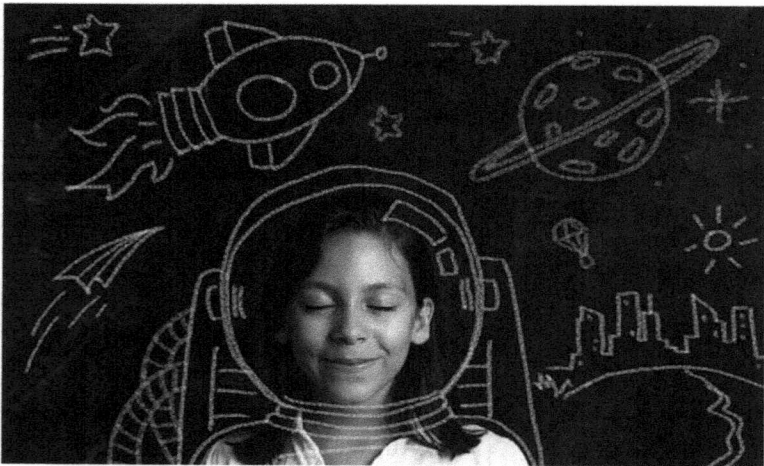

SAY IT WITH ME
"MY MIND IS A FERTILE GROUND FOR ALL OF MY DREAMS AND ASPIRATIONS"

PRINCIPLE #6
CONNECTION

"If You Want To Go Fast, Go Alone. If You Want To Go Far, Go Together"

African Proverb

Take a moment to think about the word "CONNECTION".

What does "CONNECTION" mean to you?

What else?

What else?...

Did you know that people who live longer have healthy relationships and a strong support system of people who support them?

You can watch this TED TALK video for more information:

https://www.ted.com/talks/susan_pinker_the_secret_to_living_longer_may_be_your_social_life/up-next

"It takes a village to raise a child" African Proverbs I really believe that anything is possible when we learn to work together after all teamwork makes the dream work:

https://www.youtube.com/watch?v=RqTxNrE1mfE

"It takes a village to raise a child" is an African proverb which means that it takes an entire community of different people to raise a child, form identity etc.

Did you know that people with strong and broad social relationships are happier, healthier and live longer?

Do some research to see what you can learn.

Did you also know that close relationships with family and friends provide love, meaning, support and increase our feelings of self-worth?

I have learned that broader networks bring a sense of belonging. Take a moment to think about the life you have and what you choose to create for your future.

Who do you need to become to create your dream future?

Who do you dream of being around?

What do you enjoy doing?

Did you know that taking action to strengthen our relationships and build connections is essential for our own happiness?

Humans beings are social creatures by nature and when we are with others who love and care about us it keeps us healthy.

Having healthy relationships with our parents, friends, neighbours, peers etc and people within your community is the difference that makes the difference because it is the path to happiness for them and you. The quality and quantity of social connections that we have, has a huge impact on our health and happiness as well as psychological well-being.

Did you know that when you do not have the above it has a very negative effect on our health, happiness and psychological well-being?

It is very important to have a positive, caring, supportive, loving, compassionate and understanding network of social connections or high levels of social support can increase our immunity to infection, lower our risk of heart disease and reduce mental decline as we get older.

My family and I once watch a YouTube video of an elderly care home who bring young and old together because of the benefits:
https://youtu.be/3LGSfgOi9UU

It is really important to have close, secure and supportive relationships, whether these are with our families and/or friends.

Always remember that it is the quality of our relationships that matters most.

In our family we enjoy experiencing enjoyment, fun, excitement, talking openly, feeling understood, giving and receiving of support, shared activities and experiences etc.

Always remember that relationships are a two-way thing, so you have to be willing to give and take from time to time.

The relationships we have in our lives tell us a lot about ourselves and areas that need healing. Take a moment to think about the relationships that you have with family and friends.

The question is how do you feel about the 5 people that you spend the most time with?

What do you like about each of those relationships?

What would you like to change?

What would you like to do more of with them?

What do you need to stop doing with them?

What do you need to start doing with them?

What do you need to do less of?

What do you appreciate about them?

Relationships help to make us happier and healthier.

Did you know that working on our relationships is good for our happiness and working on our happiness is good for our relationships?

In my eye, That's a win all round!
WIN-WIN-WIN!
If you WIN, then I WIN and WE BOTH WIN!
What do you think? Let's root for each other and watch each other grow.

We are social beings, take a moment to reflect on your emotions and behaviours such as compassion, love, kindness, gratitude, generosity, smiling, cuddling and laughing etc.

Have you ever taken a moment to think about the pain people go through when they have to break a bond with a loved one?

We all have a deep need to feel connected to each other and when this need is not fulfilled we fill disconnected.

This is because we need to love and be loved,

to care and be cared

When you know that you are loved and love someone, how does that make you feel?

When you know that you are cared for and have someone to care for, how does that make you feel?

I believe that it is really important to have close relationships with different people from different cultures because this helps us to expand our awareness.

Did you know that healthy relationships provide us with a sense of belonging and influence how safe and secure we feel?

I really, really, really, really believe that by building healthy relationships with family, friends and in our local community will contribute to our own happiness and people around us, enabling ourselves, families, friends and our communities to flourish.

A smile, kindness and happiness can be contagious. By smiling at others, being kind to someone and just by being happy around others can create a huge ripple effect of positivity and inspire others to do the same or **better**.

Together, WE can help to build happier families, friendships and communities by doing what we can to boost our own happiness and also being conscious of the impact that our words and behaviours may have on others.

Me and my family have an amazing program called DREAMING BIG TOGETHER.

Which aims to teach you and your family to work together to create generational success, financial and time freedom.

Always remember that even a so called seemingly small interaction, such as a friendly smile or act of kindness can have a huge impact.

The difference that makes the difference, is us being the change that we want to see in the world.

Say it with me:

"I AM ENOUGH"

say this as many times a day as you can
until your mind agrees (try it for at least 30 days).

TREAT OTHERS THE WAY YOU LIKE TO BE TREATED.

OUR BEN SALMI FAMILY BELIEFS & OUR FAMILY ANTHEM

"BEN SALMI TEAMWORK, MAKES THE DREAMWORK

We believe that there is no such thing as failure only feedback. We also believe that the journey of one-thousand miles begins with a single step

Family Anthem:

If you want to be somebody,
If you want to go somewhere,
You better wake up and

PAY ATTENTION!

I'm ready to be somebody,
I'm ready to go somewhere,
I'm ready to wake up and

PAY ATTENTION!

The question is ARE YOU"

PRINCIPLE #7
CONTRIBUTION

Take a moment to think about the word "CONTRIBUTION".

What does "CONTRIBUTION" mean to you?

What else?

What else?...

I truly believe that it is very important to have an understanding of our basic human needs, in order to feel happy and fulfilled in life.

Did you know that we all have basic human needs?

Here are some of our basic human needs (Yes food, water and a home are also important), did you know the following basic human needs?

- Certainty: Is a desire for a guaranteed outcome that will either create pain or pleasure
- Praise: Is a desire to feel acknowledged and respected
- Uncertainty: Is a desire for change.
- Contribution: Is a desire to be of service to others.
- Encouragement: Is a desire to feel supported
- Connection: Is a desire to connect with others and not feel alone.
- Love: Is a desire to give and to receive love.

55

- Safety: Is a desire to feel safe and protected.
- Significance: Is a desire to feel important and seen as a unique, special and worthy individual.
- Growth: Is a desire to obtain knowledge for example embarking on a journey of self-discovery.

I think praise, encouragement, certainty, uncertainty, contribution, connection, love, safety and growth make us feel good and when we learn to find healthy ways to fulfil these basic needs this is the difference that makes the difference in our lives.

Ask yourself, how do you currently fulfil your needs for each of the above?

If you fulfil some of your basic needs in an un-healthy way, what can you choose to do differently?

Just for the record we all need food, water and a home to live in. The above needs are different to these, I am sharing what we learned at personal development events.

Did you know that to be of service to others is like being of service?

When you are of service to others, your act of service goes on to touch the lives of many because good deeds inspire others to say and do the same or better.

Did you know that the desire for contribution/acts of service for others is one of our basic human needs?

Did you know that by contribution into the lives of others can have a positive effect on our bodies?

Do some research because there are studies that show that when people donated to charities etc, their mesolimbic system (the part of our brain responsible for <u>feelings of reward</u>) is triggered.

The brain also releases feel-good chemicals which inspires you to be of service to others more often.

Leading experts explain that as feelings of social connectedness increase, and so does your confidence. By contributing to others, you will boost your confidence.

Being of service to others can help to build stronger friendships, and by being a positive support system in someone else's life can <u>build a long-lasting bond</u>.

When you help others, you give off positive vibes, which can also rub off on your peers and improve your relationships and contribute towards maintaining a mutually, beneficial positive dynamics.

Did you know that people who contribute in the lives of other have been found to have a higher self-esteem and overall well-being?

Take a moment to think about the different ways that you currently contribute in the lives of others?

Did you know that helping others can make you feel like a SUPER HERO?

What do you feel when you positively contribute in the lives of others?

I love people so much, I really enjoy helping others because I can. I love helping people because it feels good and when I help others I am being the change that I want to see in the world.

Helping others keeps me healthy because I help others because my cup is overflowing with love so much so that I just have to **share** the **love** with others. I really believe that by having a positive impact on someone else could help YOU to change your own outlook and attitude towards life and people around you.

Contribution can help to reduce stress, sadness, loneliness and isolation.

And it will boost your self-confidence, inner peace, improve your mood and eventually make you feel more optimistic, fulfilled, grateful, empowered, inspired, positive and also enrich your sense of purpose in life.

Did you know that when you help others, you can also learn how to help yourself?

Sometimes when we have problems we might say something like this to ourselves "Why does this always happen to me", "I am the only one suffering", "I always get things wrong" etc. Because we sometimes believe that we are the only person experiencing that problem.

My mum always says, "Life is merely a journey of market research and what we choose to do with the research is up to us" and "Things don't just happen to you, because you can also choose to believe that they happen for you", "Whenever a challenge presents, we can say it is merely contrast. That then gives you a choice to choose what you desire to experience next".

The truth is each and every problem we have someone else has experienced it too.

So, when you help others you can also learn how they overcame your own problem, appreciate life more, know that we are enough, learn how to cope and grow through the experience.

Helping others can empower us to solve our own problems. If you've never been through a tough experience or just have a case of the blues, being of service to others is a great way to step into your power.

Me and my family once watched a movie called
Pay It Forward.
The movie taught me how powerful each and every one
of us are (yes, I am talking to YOU – because YOU
ARE ENOUGH!!..).
By watching the movie, I also learned that one act of
kindness has the power to transform the lives of others
and the entire world.

I challenge you to do at least three kind things to three
people that you see during the next 24 hours. If they
thank you and ask how they can repay you, or why you
did it just say

*"Because I can and now you can choose to
PAY IT FORWARD – because together we can
make the world a better place one good deed at a
time"*

Then just smile!

Always remember that there is no good deed to big or
too small. You could smile at someone, compliment
someone, help someone to solve a problem, hold a door
open for others as you enter a door.

Simply say and/or do whatever feels in alignment and
what feels good at the time.

Our family mentor #1 FEMALE ENTREPRENUR

Regan Ann Hillyer (one of the most successful Business Woman in the world), always says:

"You absolutely can have it all" and "Do what feels GOOD and what feels in alignment"

PRINCIPLE #8
I LOVE MYSELF

Take a moment to think about "SELF LOVE".

What does "SELF LOVE" mean to you?

What else?

What else?...

Learning to love yourself is really important, especially if you choose to have a happier lifestyle.

Did you know that when you learn how to love yourself, you stop worrying what other people think and say about you?

BEING YOU IS A PIECE OF CAKE POEM

"It's good being **ME**!....

I am happy being **ME** and I'm not trying to be someone else, because I AM special and **LOVED**. That's why being **ME** is a piece of cake.

It is very important to learn to **LOVE** myself and be proud of myself about trying my best.

Being **ME** is always easier, because it is a piece of cake being **ME**.

I always try to do my best no matter what and set a good example for my peers by simply being **ME**".

**Well done for acknowledging
how special YOU are xxx
(SMILE) xxx**

Always know that you are precious and loved dearly.
BY THE WAY the fact that you are alive means that you are special.

"YOU ARE ENOUGH!..."

"No one can walk your walk, no one can dance your dance and no one can sing your song "
Lashai Ben Salmi
(My big Sister)

DRIP DROP POEM

Drip, drop, drip, drop........
I run down the window......
As a single pure seed and when connected I begin to grow.

Drip, drop, drip, drop........
I'm invincible, I can move through form and out of form based upon my heart's desire.

Drip, drop, drip, drop........
Although there are millions of rain drops on the window, I stand as one and I am unique.....

Drip, drop, drip, drop........
One day my drip, drop, drip, drop may appear to be gone, however the trail I leave behind shall always be remembered. What trail will your drip, drop, drip, drop be remembered for? What seed will you plant today?

By Lashai Ben Salmi
(My big Sister)

LEARN TO LOVE 'YOU'

Life can present a range of fear provoking and exhilarating thoughts!
It is entirely normal to experience mixed emotions from time to time.
There will be days when you feel: confident, playful and happy.

There will also be days when you feel: sad, discontent and miserable. Days when you are not feeling 100% - it's particularly important to wear a huge **(SMILE)**!

Be kind and loving towards yourself just as you would be towards **LOVED** ones.

Do things to make you feel good for example listen to music, talk to friends and family, draw, look into a mirror and appreciate yourself, write, laugh, read or exercise - whatever makes you feel good

JUST DO IT!

Express gratitude for your life and praise yourself for all your achievements. For example, you could say "I am so proud of myself for: completing my homework, helping out around the house or reading a book".
Whatever it is**(((CELEBRATE)))** your achievements throughout the day.

These sentences can help to make you feeling good:

- I **LOVE** being me
- I **LOVE** my life
- I **LOVE** my perfect body
- I **LOVE** being healthy
- I am the man (for boys only!)
- I am beautiful (for girls only!)
- I **LOVE** my happiness and soooooooooo much more
- I **LOVE** being ME... I **LOVE** being ME... I **LOVE** being ME...! YIPPEE! YIPPEE! YIPPEE!

(SMILE) I **LOVE** my life...

by Lashai Ben Salmi
(My big Sister)

I love being me, and I love the family that I have especially my big sister Lashai Ben Salmi because she has taught me so many things, that I never knew that existed. She is my role model and I'm not just going to say my role model, not like anyone else.
She is a very special role model to me.

Lashai Ben Salmi my big sister if you are reading this or listening to this I am telling you right now and right in these very pages you are amazing, you are clever, I love you so much, you are beautiful, you are the sister that everyone in the world has dreamed of having.

Thank you for loving me and being my big sister. Thank you Lashai for all that you have done for me and especially for teaching me to speak Korean.

Thank you, thank you, thank you God. I just want to say that I also love and appreciate my three brothers Tray-Sean, Paolo and Amire too.

I love being me, because I get to choose all the things that I want to do in life. I love being me because I have people in my life who love and care about me. I love my life because I have a loving, caring and supportive family who helped me through my life journey and to reach my dreams. I have a DREAM to help people around the world, by helping them to find their happiness and to find their inner child hidden deep within their soul.

Did you know that your values and beliefs are learned from a combination of your family, friends, religion, school, geography, demographics, economics, media and significant emotional events?

- Do you know how powerful your brain is?

- Do you **know** how your unconscious minds absorb information from birth?

Between the ages of 0-7 your brain is like a sponge and you copy whatever you are exposed to.
This is known as the 'Imprint Period'.

Between the ages of 7-14 you begin to select role models, and this is **know**n as the 'Modelling Period'.

Between the ages of 14-21 you choose a group to belong to. It is fair to say that this group became your life advisory board in many ways. This is **known** as the 'Socialization Period'.

Between the ages of 21-35 is when you would have gathered a collection of experiences as a result of all of the above. It is believed that to some extent your 'Business Persona' resembles your first boss of authority figure. This is known as the 'Business Persona Period'.

Did you know, where your attention goes, energy flows and results will show?

Your beliefs are possibilities which you believe to be true.
Your beliefs are 'Your Boundary Conditions'.
Your beliefs change your capabilities, behaviour and the environment you choose to be in.

Change your beliefs and you can change your life.
Your capabilities are influenced by your behaviour.

When you enhance your capabilities, your behaviour will improve, and change will happen.

Your behaviour is influenced by your capabilities, and will affect the environment which you choose to be in.

Changing your environment has less of an impact on changing your life because it is a superficial change because it is not deep rooted enough to cause a significant change.

I hope you took that all in **S.M.I.L.E.**

<u>S</u>ee <u>M</u>iracles <u>I</u>n <u>L</u>ife <u>E</u>verywhere

take a moment to think about these questions:

- Where do you believe you learned some of your behaviours from?

The good news is, if you learned unfulfilling behaviours.
You can choose to learn more fulfilling ones, right?
Is that a YES or NO? Ha, ha, ha!

- Did you **know** that your brain processes information using representational systems after receiving data from your five senses?

These senses are sight, sound, touch, taste, smell and self-talk.

Your brain translates the external world into an internal representation of your own unique reality, as we all have our own interpretation of reality.

Did you know that when we love ourselves?

- We let go of blame, shame and anger.

- We invite ownership, creativity and power into our lives

- We feel, hear, and believe in our own inner power

- The opinion of others doesn't matter

- We care most about what we think about ourselves

- We feel at peace within ourselves

- We accept ourselves unconditionally

- We know that WE ARE ENOUGH

- We take responsibility for our lives

- We recognize that we are the source of our own happiness

- We know that we can choose happiness, no matter what is happening in our life

- We let go of loneliness and embrace a deeper connection and sense of oneness with the world

When you choose to love yourself, you allow ourselves to show up in the world and love themselves too. Because you do not feel unloved so you are not scared of them loving themselves. The more YOU look at yourself with love, the more YOU practice love and acceptance toward others

YOU can let go of thoughts that are negative when you learn to love yourself. Take some time to look into a mirror. Look straight into your own eyes and say:

- "I AM are enough"

- "I Love YOU"

- "I AM worthy"

- "I AM special"

- "There is greatness in ME"

- "I forgive MYSELF"

- "I choose happiness"

- "THANK YOU"

- "I AM Sorry"

Did you know that when you choose to love yourself, you allow yourself to be human?

YOU accept mistakes and failures, and allow yourself to become vulnerable. The need to prove yourself to others will simply melt away like ice left out in the sunshine on a hot and sunny day.

All of this is possible when you choose to accept that YOU are enough.

When you choose to be loving and kind towards yourself you will stop allowing fear to rule your life, because you are choosing to lead by love instead.

Did you know that when YOU let go of competition and comparing yourself to others? You can unleash your unlimited potential to creativity, inspiration, openness and learn accept ourselves instead of blaming and fighting others. This allow us to attract harmony, peace, respect, and significance in our relationships.

When you choose love, you find the courage to accept that there is no such thing as failure, only feedback.

Each time something does not work out the way you wanted, you can choose to say, "I have just learned another way that doesn't work and I am getting closer to finding out what does work because this is taking me one step closer" because this is growth.

You will realise that your significance isn't dependent on what you have or what you produce, because you are enough just the way you are.

When we choose to love ourselves, we let go of the need to play small in this world and allow ourselves to grow. When my family and I went to an Andy Harrington Event, he often asked the audience:

"Why are YOU trying to fit in,

when YOU were born to

STAND OUT?"

I really, really, really, really love this question, please take a moment to think about this question, because when we play small we are not benefiting ourselves or anyone else. What I mean by playing small is not believing in ourselves, our dreams and our abilities.

Instead we pretend that we don't have dreams and just because we are too scared that we will be rejected, be judged or because we are too scared of failing.

For example, take a moment to imagine a tree.

It can either grow tall and large enough to provide shade and food for people or it can choose to stay small and only provide shade and food for insects. And the same goes for us in life, because the more YOU grow, the more YOU can spread love, kindness and joy in the world.

Did you know that something very powerful happens when we choose to love ourselves?

We become aware of our negative thoughts, we question them because we know they are not true and then we choose to turn them into a positive thought or affirmation for example

"This waiting line is too long to get into this theme park"

can be exchanged for

"Oh wow, I am so excited about being here because I am going to have so much fun with my family and friends when we get inside the theme park"

When you choose to love yourself unconditionally, you will begin to feel safe, you will shine naturally without having to work hard for it, you will move from scarcity to abundance in all areas of your life, you have a new understanding of rejection because you will choose to see it as a redirection. You will no longer be fearful of change, you will become conscious of the things you spend your time on, your priorities can change because what's important to you also changes.

When you choose to love yourself, you will be less judgmental of others. This will help you to realize that your values and beliefs are simply different and that's okay. Self-love helps you to treat others with the same level of respect that you like to be treated with.

Part of loving yourself is doing what you want to do. Self-love will empower you to create amazing experiences in your life. When you learn to love yourself unconditionally, what others want you to be, do and have will no longer matter. Because you'll know that your decisions are based on your own values, beliefs and goals.

IT FEELS GOOD TO BE ME & I LOVE MYSELF

WHAT ARE YOU EXCITED ABOUT IN LIFE?

WHAT MAKES YOU JUP FOR JOY?

PRINCIPLE #9
DANCE, SING, SMILE, LAUGH & CUDDLE

Take a moment to think about
"DANCING, SINGING, SMILING, LAUGHING AND
CUDDLING".

What does "DANCING, SINGING, SMILING, LAUGHING
AND CUDDLING" mean to you?

What else?

What else?...

Dancing, Singing, Smiling, laughing and cuddling are things that people need to do daily. Dancing, Singing, Smiling, laughing and cuddling are important because they will make you feel happier and have a positive impact of your physical and mental health.

Spend quality time with yourself, your family and your friends dancing, singing, smiling, laughing and cuddling. You should always, always and always cuddle together, so that the person you are cuddling knows that you love them and that deep down inside that you care for them in a very special way. It is very important for people in your life to know that you appreciate them.

When we love someone, it is important to express our love and care for them as much as possible.

I made up a speech because my soul tells me that it is a very powerful speech that needs to be shared with others, so hopefully you will enjoy it, here I go:

"Show that you have appreciation for what you have, because there will come a time when you no long have an opportunity to do so. If you only love what loves you, is that love? If you only appreciate, what appreciates you is that appreciation? If you only respect what respects you is that really respect? Just imagine how you will feel when you learn how to give without the need to receive. What you say and do is your choice so please do not follow the example of someone who has not chosen love, because that will never lead you to happiness.

If you don't be respectful to someone or something you can never love or be respectful to yourself at the same time. Because the love you give to others is because your cup is over flowing with love".

What I am trying to tell you is that no matter what a person has done to hurt you always choose to forgive because it will free you. When we do not forgive others, we hurt ourselves not them. You deserve to live a full and happy life. If you don't respect others you cannot never love and respect yourself unconditionally.

I always used to think that people say a lot but don't always do what they say.

Well you can you can say a lot of things and admit that you will say it but sometimes some people just don't keep their word and they forget how important their word was to the person who they made the promise to.

When you see your family or a friend sitting alone and looking a little lost by them-selves you should go to them and give them a nice warm hug/cuddle, dance with them, sing with them, smile with them and laugh because quality time with loved ones is priceless.

Did you know that cuddling releases oxytocin, which is also known as the feel-good hormone?

Did you know that dancing, singing, smiling, laughing and cuddling can make you feel happier?

Did you know that physical contact with others can help to reduce stress?

Did you know that when you cuddle someone you can communicate better?

Did you know that dancing can improve the condition of your heart, lungs, coordination, agility and flexibility?

Did you know that dancing can improve mental functioning, general and psychological well-being, self-confidence and social skills?

Did you know that singing can strengthen your immune system, improve your posture and can help you to sleep better?
Singing is a natural anti-depressant, singing lowers stress levels, improves mental alertness, can widen your circle of friends and it can boost your confidence.

Did you know that singing can broadens your communication skills?

Did you know that smiling can Improves your mood, lower blood pressure and it is a form of stress relief?

Smiling can improve your relationships, strengthen your Immune Function, it's a form of pain relief and smiling can extend your life?

Did you know that laughing can lower your blood pressure, reduce stress, and it can also improve your cardiac health?

Laughing improves your overall well-being and triggers the release of endorphins and boosts T-Cells (T-cells are specialized immune system cells just waiting in your body for activation). After all this research, I feel like a doctor... When you laugh, you activate T-cells that immediately begin to help you fight off sickness.)?

So, next time you feel a cold coming on, add laughing to your list for illness prevention and healing.

Learn to dance like no one is watching, sing like no one is listen, smile because your is over flowing with love, laugh out aloud because it feels good and cuddle without needing a reason to do so, did it just because you can!

I LOVE MY LIFE, I LOVE MYBODY AND I CHOOSE HAPPINESS BECAUSE I CAN.

THE QUESTION IS WHAT WILLL YOU CHOOSE TO DO DIFFERENTLY NOW?

PRINCIPLE #10
VISUALISE

Vision is one of the last and most important, important ones, because it teaches you that you have to look at your future and try to make it a better future by looking at what you can change don't waste time saying what your future is going to look like whilst you can spend your time making an even better one by finishing what you already started.

Take a moment to think about the word "VISUALISE".

What does "VISUALISE" mean to you?

What else?

What else?...

I really, really, really, really enjoy visualising achieving my dreams, because it makes me feel good when I AM experiencing my dreams over and over and over again.

It is so much fun to visualise, all you need to do it take some time to sit down to think about your dream and can write it down if you would like to describe your dream in more details.

Visualisation process

(please read this a couple of times until you understand and then enjoy the experience to see how it feels):

In order to begin, you need to be relaxed.

May you please sit down or lay down in a comfortable position.

Now take three deep breathes

Slowly breathe in to fill your lungs and chest with air, breathe in.......... and breathe out..............., breathe in.............. and breathe out..........., breathe in.......... and breathe out...............

Well done, now let's start the visualisation process.

Visualize yourself experiencing your dream happier lifestyle......... See what you see, hear what you hear, feel what you feel and become aware of where you are, what you are doing and who you are doing it with...

Yes, that's right it feels so good now that you are living your dream. Now Imagine yourself experiencing joy, excitement, adventure, fun and so much more

Can you see that, yes that's right it feels good to be YOU?

Listen to what people around you are saying and just look at their faces beaming back at you with such pride and appreciation of you. Notice how you feel inside after seeing the positive way that people are reacting to you.

Visualize and feel yourself fully connected to this experience so much so that you say to yourself

"Oh yeah, I knew I could do it and it feels amazing. It's done, it's done, it's done – momentum, momentum, momentum."

Take a moment to notice what you are wearing and how it makes you feels. Continue to notice how positively people are responding to you now that you have chosen to step into your power and live your dream lifestyle.

Now all you need to do is preserve the positive learnings for yourself and for the future because now that you know how good it feels to live your dream lifestyle all you now have to do is, choose to step into your power now!!

Please take 3 deep breaths and just wiggle your toes and fingers and allow yourself to become fully present within this room

Well done you were amazing – how was that experience for you?

You may like to take notes

Now do this breathing technique to submit this positive experience into your mind.

4 Seconds
- Take 3 deep breathes and then relax
- Now take a slow and controlled deep breath in to the count of 4 seconds
- And then hold your breath for 4 seconds
- Now breath out slowly to the count of 4 seconds

6 Seconds
- Now take a slow and controlled deep breath in to the count of 6 seconds
- And then hold your breath for 6 seconds
- Now breath out slowly to the count of 6 seconds

8 Seconds
- Now take a slow and controlled deep breath in to the count of 8 seconds
- And then hold your breath for 8 seconds
- Now breath out slowly to the count of 8 seconds

Well done

Have you heard of the saying "Seeing Is Believing"

Before we can believe in a goal, we usually have to see it first either by observing someone else's life experience or by visualisation.

Visualisation comes is a simple technique that allows you to create a mental image of a future event.

When my family and I watched the movie 'The Secret', we learned that our brains cannot tell the difference between reality and visualisation because the same part of the brain is stimulated for both.

Did you know that when we visualise our desired outcome, we begin to "see" the possibility of achieving it?

Through visualisation we experience our dreams, this inspires us to take action.

Visualization is a proven and well-developed technique that produces results when practice regularly every day and it is used by some of the most successful people around the world. Men and women or boys and girls.

Did you know that visualisation works because the same neurons in our brains activate when we visualise and when we have the actual experience?

Visualisation alone does not guarantee success, and it will not replace having to take physical action, commitment, practice and hard work hard.

However, when you combine visualisation with a good network of support, mentors, coaches and a big why, then the easier the how – then it is a powerful way to achieve positive change towards creating your dreams.

S.M.I.L.E.
See Miracles In Life Everywhere

Make your own S.M.I.L.E. acronym

S :

M :

I :

L :

E :

CONGRATULATIONS – WELL DONE FOR LEARNING THE 10 KEY PRINCIPLES TO CREATE A HAPPIER LIFESTYLE

SURPRISE BONUS ACTIVITIES TO SUIT DIFFERENT LOVEPRENURE PERSONALITIES

Indoor Activities for Homebound LovePrenures

- Build an indoor obstacle course
- Play chess
- Exercise
- Read
- Create your own puzzle
- Find an age appropriate tutorial on YouTube (ask for your parents for their permission)
- Ask an adult to help you to rearrange your bedroom
- Play some music and dance like no one is watching
- Play Simon Says
- Create a performance to share with your family

Innovative Actives for Innovative LovePrenures

- Act out your favourite book
- Write your own book
- Come up with a business idea
- Do some baking (ask an adult to help with the oven and any dangerous equipment)
- Bring out the pots and pans and practice drumming skills.
- Build new structures and objects out of LEGOs (without using the instructions).
- Compose a poem
- Create a community project to help others in need
- Design -- and fill in -- your own mad libs.
- Publish a pretend newspaper.
- Write a gratitude letter to someone special to express how much you appreciate them (e.g. your parents, siblings, grandparents etc

Food Focused Activates for Master Chef LovePrenures

- Bake cookies
- Cook an entire meal ask your parents to help
- Bake bread
- Make homemade ice cream
- Bake Fairy cakes
- Bake muffins
- Make vegetable and fruit smoothies Yummy…. yum… yum…

Active Activities for Active LovePrenures

- Spend the day at your local swimming pool
- Go to a mini golf course
- Go karting
- Play football
- Play basketball
- Play tennis
- Ride a bike
- Play catch
- Roller skate
- Roller blade.
- Run relay races
- Spend the day in the park
- Throw around the Frisbee with some friends

Thought Provoking Activities for Child Genius LovePrenures

- Write an A4 page detailing the lifestyle you desire to create when you grow up
- Research experts in an industry that interests you
- Explore the world with <u>Google Maps</u> (ask for your parents' permission first)
- Do some research at your local library (ask your parent to take you)
- Teach yourselves Sign Language (ASL) alphabet.
- Visit an interactive museum.

This is a photo of the 20 Finalist of Channel 4 Child Genius 2017.

My older brother, Tray-Sean is on the back-row top right hand corner, with Richard Osman was one of them!

I am so proud of him, my big BRO!

Creative Activities for Creative LovePrenures

- Blow homemade bubble (find the step by step online)
- Make a sun dial
- Create bubble paint prints
- Draw cool murals
- Give your parents a make over
- Create a flower arrangement for the dining room table.
- Take creative photos indoors and outdoors
- Tie-dye a T-shirt!

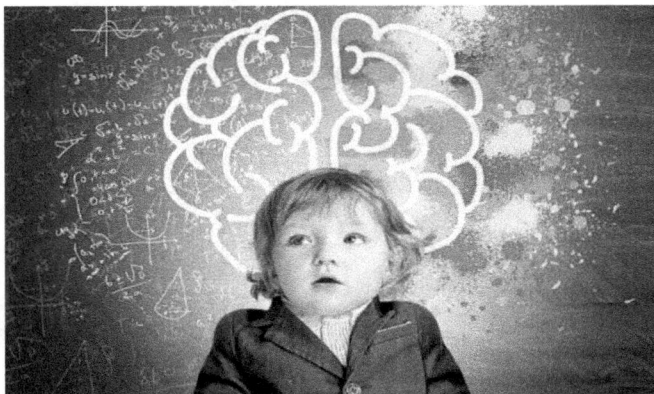

Exploration Activities for Adventurous Loveprenures

- Visit your local farmers' market and discover interesting products you've never seen before.
- Put together some items to put into a time capsule and bury it in your garden
- Set up a lemonade stand.
- Visit www.365tickets.com for an adventurous day out with your family
- Visit www.kidzania.co.uk to plan a fun day out with your family
- Ask your parents to visit www.merlinannualpass.co.uk to purchase an annual pass for your family (come up with some ideas to raise the money to pay for the tickets)

Now I want you to choose to feel
AMAZINGLY HAPPY
NOW
AND
GO AFTER
YOUR DREAMS!

YASMINE BEN SALMI

"The choice is yours, the question is what will you now choose to say and do?"

Yasmine Ben Salmi
Award winning Author of
The Choice is Your
- 10 Key Principles To Create A Happier Lifestyle.
Winner of TruLittle Heros Award - Creative
2017, Former International Radio Show Host.
Founder of Loveprenure. Yasmine is here to help you
to plant the seed for wealth, health and happiness in
abundance via a variety of products and services to
assist you to create a brighter future.

Yasmine is the middle child of five siblings: LASHAI, TRAY-SEAN, PAOLO and AMIRE

Together they are known as

"The Fantastic Five"

I KNOW
YOU ARE
AWESOME!

I hope one day I can meet you.

NOW MY FAMILY
ARE GOING
TO SHARE
SOME BONUS INFORMATION
WITH
YOU

BONUS SURPRISE - MUSIC

Did you know that *MUSIC* appeals to your ever emotion? It soothes and excites you, uplifts and inspires you. It moves you to happiness and reduces you to tears because music speaks directly to your hearts.

- Can you imagine life without music?

- Have you ever wondered how different genre of music influences your mood or actions?

- What is your favourite genre of music and how does it make you feel when you listen to it?

- Observe your friends, family and other people you know. Observe the music they listen to and how do you think that genre of music influences their mood or behaviour?

- Have you ever noticed how some music makes you feel playful, aggressive or even sad?

10 Things You Should Know About Your Brain

FACT 1: There are always 4 Stages of Learning

Stage One – UNCONSCIOUS INCOMPETENCE

This is when you start doing something new so doing it by 'Trial and Error' and hoping for the better!

Stage Two – CONSCIOUS INCOMPETENCE

This is the 'MAKE or BREAK' stage and often 95% people will give up at this stage if they don't get success and will NEVER discover their potential! So, it is vital to get a Mentor, Coach or an Instructor. For example, if you want to learn to drive a car then book a serious of lessons with a Qualified Instructor.

Stage Three – CONSCIOUS COMPETENCE

Yeah! You can do it! Like after a number of lessons you know how to drive a car but you still need to think of everything you are doing to drive the car safely!

Stage Four: UNCONSCIOUS COMPETENCE
You have Mastered the skill because you had so much practice and can do it without thinking about it.

FACT TWO: We all have a Preferred Learning Style known as V.A.K.

V – VISUAL (We like to learn by Reading or Looking at the information);

A – AUDITORY (We like to learn by Listening or Talking);

K – KINESTHETICS (We like to learn by Doing and Active).

To increase our skills factor, ideally, we want to develop over time all three V, A and K!

FACT THREE: We actually have 5 Types of W.I.R.E.S. Memory

W – WORKING MEMORY (Short Term Memory)

I – IMPLICIT MEMORY (Or sometimes called 'The Muscle' memory. Once you have learned to do something, like how to use a new computer software etc.)
R – REMOTE (This is your lifetime accumulation of skills and knowledge and seems to diminish with age if you don't use it! "USE IT or LOST IT!")

E - EPISODIC

FACT FOUR: Learn to Search and Recognized for

Patterns enhances Brain development.

FACT FIVE: Your ability to learn is 'State' dependent. So, have a High Expectation when you learn you will succeed.

FACT SIX: Emotions and Learning are closely linked.

Watch what you are saying to yourself when learning.
Have a high expectation of yourself.
Don't say: "I will never be able to learn all these things!"
Instead, say something like: "Everything I learned, I will remember at the right time to use."

FACT SEVEN: We all have 'DUEL' Daily Learning cycles

The two cycles are: "Low to high energy" and "Relaxation to Tension" Cycle.
So be aware of your best time for learning, especially for test revision.

FACT EIGHT: Our brain modal switch over roughly every 90 minutes.
Generally speaking, our left brain is more efficient for verbal skills and our right brain for spatial skills.

FACT NINE: Our Learning and Physical performance is affected by our biological rhythms throughout the day.

Even our breathing has cycles.

Overall, short term memory is best in the morning and not so effective in the afternoon.
Whilst our long-term memory is better in the afternoon.

FACT TEN: Your brain needs Deep Relaxing sleep. This allows time for your brain to process all the things you have learned.
Getting into a REM sleep (Dreaming) has been found by researchers to be very important for learning.

SURPRISE BONUS: EARTHING

Did you know that walking barefoot in soil can actually decrease white blood cell count and increase red blood cell count which can result in a positive immune response?

Did you know that walking barefoot can also reduce the risk of heart dis-ease?

The correct name for walking barefoot in soil is called Earthing. Walking barefoot also decreases the feeling of anxiety and stress and regulates your nervous system

Did you know that just going outside to get some fresh air can help to regulate your emotions and balance your nervous system?

And when you choose to let your body connect with the soil can have a host of positive emotional and health benefits.

This is because the soil carries a negative charge and we have a positive charge due to all the electromagnetic waves we come in contact with every daily, so it is a really good idea to spend as much time as possible out in nature and walking barefoot.

WALKING BAREFOOT

CAN STRENGTHEN

YOUR

IMMUNE SYSTEM

Surprise Bonus: DID YOU KNOW?

Did YOU know that we all develop our belief systems about ourselves and the world around us from our environment?

Our family and friends, role models, television, magazines and advertising can either be nurturing or damaging.

It is important that we, our families and our friends learn to take control of our belief systems and the younger that we do, the easier it is.

It can be as simple as affirming the positive beliefs that we would like to grow up with. Negative beliefs can impact our lives greatly and can be hard to shift as we grow older.

Affirmations are a powerful and holistic way of building positive mind and happier children and will go onto help them through their lives.

This will also nurture their authentic self and help them to enjoy the magic of childhood.
Put simply, Because I Am Intelligent - 365 Affirmations To Brighten Up Your Day aims to affirm to one's self positive words that are absorbed by the mind to create your belief system.

Once affirmations are learned, they work by coming to mind when that belief is challenged.

For example, if your affirmation is
"I am wonderful just the way I am",
and you are told you are stupid,
the affirmation will come to mind, to remind you of your beliefs.

Instead, you will think,
"I'm not stupid, I am wonderful!"

Without a positive belief, you may take on the one you just heard and start to believe that you are stupid. The more an affirmation is repeated, positive or negative, the stronger it becomes.

ABOUT THE BEN SALMI FAMILY

Sabrina Ben Salmi BSc
BYA Mother of The Year Award Winner

Is a proud mother of
5 Entrepreneurial children aged 4 to 17 years old
who she refers to as her

Fantastic 5.

Sabrina is a Multi-Award Winning Author, Business & Personal Development Consultant, Founding directors of an Ofsted rated Outstanding school: Harris Invictus Academy (Secondary).
Former Radio Show Host, Public Speaker. Founder of Dreaming Big Together Formula & 21 Day Shift Happens.

Sabrina Ben Salmi BSc is here to empower you to plant the seed so that you and your family can learn to Dream Big Together via a variety of products and services that aim to assist you and your loved ones to create a brighter future.

Sabrina and her children have been featured in the media Internationally via Radio, TV, Newspapers, magazines etc to name a few Channel 4 documentaries:

Secret Millionaire/Child Genius, BBC London News, LBC Radio, BBC Radio, Fabulous Magazine etc. "It's about time that we stop granting our children indefinite leave to remain on the streets and empower them to plant the seed for a brighter tomorrow"

Mohamed Ben Salmi
Is a proud father of
3 and 2 step Entrepreneurial children aged 4 to 17 years old

Speaks Arabic/French/English, author of 'A Mirror of Happiness' and has a passion for music, travel, languages, meeting new people and biology.

Lashai Ben Salmi
is a 17 years old

Multi-Award winning Youth Advocate,
Winner of TruLittle Hero Award - Entrepreneur 2017,
Speaker at Virgin Money Lounge Historical Black History Month first ever event, YouTuber 12K Subscribers plus & 2M+ views (Korean Channel), PRECIOUS Award Winner, Rotary Young Citizen Award,
Award-Winning Author of Kidz That Dream Big & Kidz book series,
Andy Harrington ACE Coach,
Former International Radio Show Host, UnLTD Award Winner,

Winner of Andy Harrington Public Speaking Awards x
2,
Harry Singha Foundation Lead Coach.
Winner of Regan Hillyer International Scholarship,
Public Speaker, Training,
Short Film: I AM A Piece To The Puzzle,
Business/Personal Developments Consultant and
Founder of My Journey - Giving Youth Several
Reasons to Smile & Put The RED CARD Up To
bullying.

She is here to help you to plant the seed for self-
realisation, personal development and happiness in
abundance via a variety of products and services to
assist you to create a brighter future.

- Mother & Daughter Discussions of Exploration
- Stepping Stones Coaching
- My Journey – Creating A Vision Board for My
Future
- My Journey – Sharing My Message from The Stage
- My Journey - Inspiring My Community To Pay It
Forward
- My Journey - There's A Book Inside ME
- Stepping Stones - Families That Play Together, Stay
Together.

Tray-Sean Ben Salmi
aka I'm That KID
is a 13 years old

Multi-Award Winning Child Advocate, participant of Child Genius 2017 1 of the final 20 smartest children in the UK,
An Award Winning Author of Kidz That Dream Big book series,
Former Radio Show Host,
Regan Hillyer International Be Your Brand Fellow,

Author of 10 Seconds To Child Genius

Events Host, UnLTD Award winner,
Nominated for National Diversity Award,
Winner of TruLittle Hero Award - Academic 2017, Public Speaker,
Business/Personal Developments Consultant and Founder of I'm That KID which offers a variety of products and services:
- I'm That KID - Bridging The Gap Between Fathers & Sons
- I'm That KID – Wristbands, Keyrings & T-Shirts
- I'm That KID – Creating A Vision Board for My Future
- I'm That KID – Taking The Stage
- I'm That KID - Inspiring My Community To Pay It Forward
- I'm That KID - There's A Book Inside ME
- I'm That KID - Families That Play Together, Stay Together
- I'm That KID - Empowering You To Step Into Your POWER

And Co-Founder of 10 Seconds To Child Genius who is here to help children and youth to plant the seed for an abundance of unique opportunities via a variety of products and services to assist you to create a brighter future.

My brother Tray-Sean Ben Salmi decided to get out of his comfort zone one day and applied to participate in Channel 4 TV 'Child Genius' competition competing against the best 8 – 12 years old in the UK and he managed to pass all their tests, interviews and assessments and made it to the Child Genius' 2017 Finals as one of the Top 20 contestants in the country.

Our family are so proud of him

**Yasmine Ben Salmi
aka LovePrenure
is an 10 years old**

Award winning Author of
The Choice is Your
- 10 Keys Principles To Create A Happier Lifestyle,

Winner of TruLittle Heros Award - Creative 2017,

Former International Radio Show Host.

Founder of Loveprenure.

Yasmine is here to help you to plant the seed for wealth, health and happiness in abundance via a variety of products and services to assist you to create a brighter future.

**Paolo Ben Salmi
aka Pint Size Adventurer
is 8 years old**

He is an Award Winning Author of Pint Size Adventurer

- 10 Keys Principles To Get Your KIDS off their iPads & Into The Wild,

2nd place in TruLittle Heros Award - U12 Entreprenur 2017,

Former International Radio Show Host,

On 22nd September 2017, Paolo made history by being the youngest to interview World Famous
Dr John Demartini:

Personal developments coach and founder of Pint Size
Adventurer who is here to help you to plant the seed
toward self-discovery, exploration of the internal and
external world and adventurer in abundance via a
variety of products and services to assist you to create
a brighter future.

Amire Ben Salmi
aka Mr Because I AM Intelligent
is a 4 years old

An Award-Winning Author of
Because I AM Intelligent
- 52 Affirmations To Brighten Up Your Day.

In 2017, he became the
YOUNGEST PUBLISHED AUTHOR IN THE
WORLD AT AGE 4!
We are waiting confirmation from
The Guinness Book of Record

Founder of Because I AM Intelligent who is here
to help you to plant the seed toward having fun
learning during childhood,
Positive Affirmations, Fun and Creativity in
abundance via a variety of products such as a
book with a matching colour car and 52

affirmation cards to assist you to create a brighter future.

YOU CAN CONNECT WITH ALL OF US ON FACEBOOK

Here's a link to a video of me board breaking at the Power to Achieve with Auntie Cheryl Chapman: https://youtu.be/fO4RmM77An8

Me being interviewed for the Gusiness Book of Records 12 minute convo with Engel Jones: http://www.twelveminuteconvos.com/875-twelve-minute-convos-w-yasmine-ben-salmi/

OUR FAMILY BELIEFS & OUR FAMILY ANTHEM

"BEN SALMI TEAMWORK, MAKES THE DREAMWORK

We believe that there is no such thing as failure only feedback.
We also believe that the journey of one-thousand miles begins with a single step

Family Anthem:

If you want to be somebody,
If you want to go somewhere,
You better wake up and

PAY ATTENTION

I'm ready to be somebody,
I'm ready to go somewhere,
I'm ready to wake up and

PAY ATTENTION!
The question is ARE YOU"

MY PRODUCTS & SERVICES

DO YOU WANT TO TAKE PART in THE
CHOICE IS YOURS 21 DAYS CHALLENGE? – Plant the seed for happiness?

21 Days – 21 Children - £21 Gift – All For A Small Investment (ask for more of details and promotional investment by quoting "THE CHOICE IS YOURS")
- You will participate in tasks designed to help you
- You will be held accountable
- You will be gifted £21 at the end of the challenge if you complete the daily challenges

For more information contact us:
- Facebook Page: Loveprenure – The choice is YOURS, always know that YOU are LOVED
- Email: yasminebensalmi2007@gmail.com
- Skype: live.yasminebensalmi2007

♥THE CHOICE IS YOURS♥ WRISTBANDS £1

GRATITUDE JAR SET £12.99

THE CHOICE IS YOURS 21 Day Skype Coaching/Mentoring for a small investment (ask for more of details and promotional investment by quoting "THE CHOICE IS YOURS") to inspire YOU to have fun learning.

HOW I MET SAM LIVERMORE

This is a letter I wrote when I was 6yrs old: Here's a link of me and Paolo being interviewed by Sam: https://youtu.be/8AKy5zIvS-k

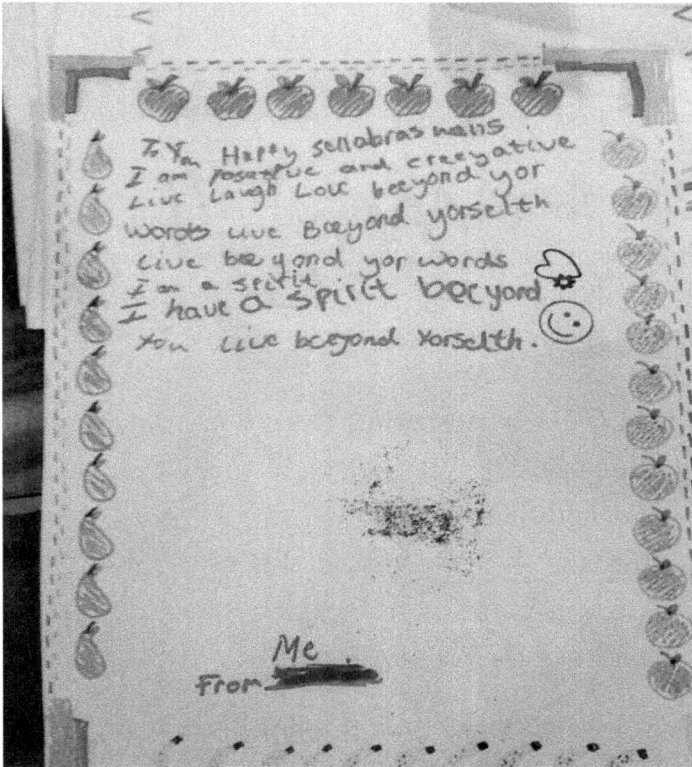

When I was about 6yrs old, me and my family went to a Mind, Body and Spirit exhibition in Earls Court.

When we arrived at the entrance there was a letter writing workshop called Love Letters. We were all told to sit down and write love letters to strangers. We were all having so much fun writing our letters.

119

When I was 6yrs old I use to love writing Angel Letters to people so I really enjoyed writing my love letter. When I finished my love letter Sam read my letter ad then asked my mum if she had helped me to write my letter, my mum said no and then Sam started to cry tears of joy.

Sam invited me, my brothers and sister to be interviewed on her YouTube channel and I told her that I would write a book called Oh! I Think I've Lost My Happiness. This book was going to be about a little girl who thank happiness was all about getting money, sweets and toys.

Until she went on a journey to find happiness and then found out that happiness is and always was inside of her heart. I asked Sam to write the book foreword for that book and she said she would. Then for one reason or another a lot of time went by and I stated to slowly write the book but I never got around to finishing it.

Then I decided to change the book title to The Choice Is Yours - 10 Key Principles To Create A Happier Lifestyle.

I am so happy that I was able to finish this book and thank you so much for writing the book foreword Sam Livermore.

Xoxo

A photo of me taken by Sam Livermore at the event

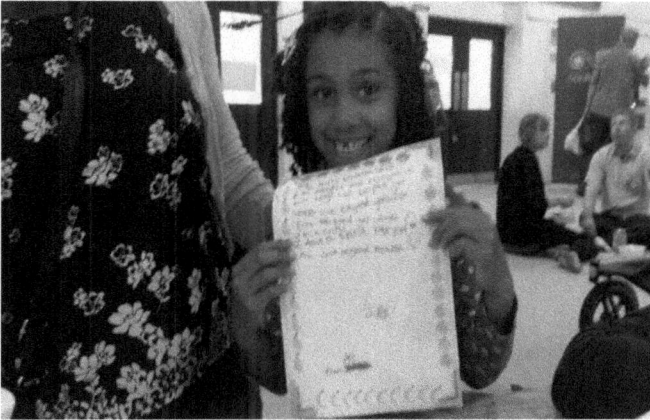

A beautiful photo frame of my Love Letter on Sam Livermore's' wall

HAPPINESS TIPS

My logo – Loveprenure is about loving yourself no matter what

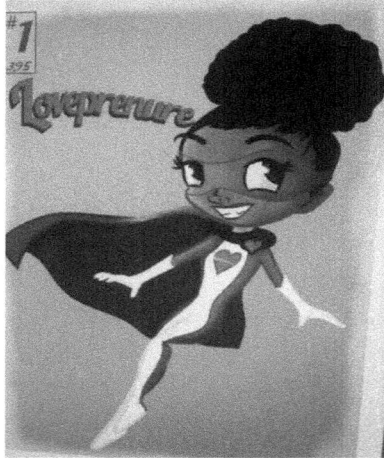

Happiness Tip #1 You are a diamond, if anyone tells you otherwise just say "I AM A Diamond and I choose to shine BRIGHT" Have faith in yourself & God always

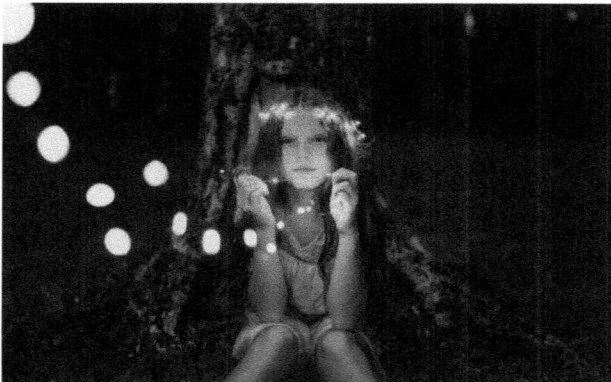

Happiness Tip #2 Go outside on an adventure and have some fun, it is good for your health and happiness

Happiness Tip#3 Drink plenty of water to be healthy and wash away any toxins and impurities

Happiness Tip #4 It is important to learn how to have fun making money. The secret to the game is to have multiple streams of income

Happiness Tip #5 Awaken the giant within, after all you are a piece to the puzzle – FIND YOUR PURPOSE and live by it

Happiness Tip #6 Spend time outside in nature, the benefits will transform your life

Happiness Tip #7 Your health is your wealth, and food is fuel so choosing to eat healthy food will keep you happy and healthy

Happiness Tip #8 Show affection and love towards others, it will make you and them happy

Happiness Tip #9 Surrender to the process and allow creativity to flow through you with ease

Happiness Tip #10 Spend quality time with people who you love and care about

Happiness Tip #11 Travel the world, to experience different languages, foods, cultures and people to help you expand your awareness of this beautiful Earth we call home

Happiness Tip #12 BE YOURSELF, BECAUSE YOU ARE ENOUGH. YOU ARE A SUPER HERO – It's time to share your SUPER POWERS with the WORLD

Happiness Tip #13 DON'T WAIT FOR THE RAIN TO STOP, LEARN TO SMILE WHATEVER THE WEATHER

Happiness Tip #14 You have something worthwhile in you, there's a book inside you and you can take to the stage to share your message. Life is a journey of market research. What you choose to do with the research is up to you.

Happiness Tip #15 Always remember that you can choose to be happy. Life has an abundance of unexpected pleasantries and you get to choose to experience them one bite at a time

A MESSAGE FROM MY HEART TO YOUR HEART, UNTIL WE MEET AGAIN

"When would now be a good idea to trust your highest thought, your clearest words and your grandest feeling? Your highest thought is always the thought which makes your feel good. Your clearest words are the words which contain truth and honesty. Your grandest feeling is *LOVE*"

Can YOU see
how much fun we have together
as a
FAMILY?

I want my BEST FRIENDS to be
my MUM, DAD
and
MY SIBLINGS.

If we can achieve this,

SO, CAN YOU!

I BELIEVE IN YOU AND WISH YOU HAPPINESS IN ABUNDANCE

"SELF LOVE IS THE ROAD TO HAPPINESS"

I hope that you enjoyed reading this book, as much as I enjoyed doing the research my family and writing this book.

Sending YOU OCEANS OF LOVE
Yasmine Ben Salmi
aka LovePrenure
www.dreamingbigtogether.com & www.10secondstochildgenius.co.uk

www.ingramcontent.com/pod-product-compliance
Lightning Source LLC
Chambersburg PA
CBHW071819090426
42737CB00012B/2143